The Modern Stoic

*Understand Ancient Stoic Philosophy and Learn
Practical Ways To Develop Perseverance, Resilience
& Calm in Today's Complex World*

(Timeless Wisdom For A Simpler Life)

Nicholas Hill

nicholashillbooks@gmail.com

Table of Contents

Introduction

When most people think of the term 'philosophy' their eyes glaze over. In fact, this the last thing they want, let alone something they need. But this is not true.

In fact, understanding and implementing the philosophy has been the way of life for men and women in our history to solve their day to day life problems as well as to achieve their biggest victories. It's not merely some rhetoric lecture given by some professors, who have merely researched the thick text books, rather the principles of the philosophy evolved through real life practical usage. In the words of Henry David Thoreau,

"To be a philosopher is not merely to have subtle thoughts, nor even to found a school...it is to solve some of the problems of life, not only theoretically, but practically."

There are many ancient philosophies that, if implemented well, can significantly improve the quality of your life. There are quite a number of ancient philosophies that are major yardsticks to the day to day activities of modern civilization. In fact, this is evident in the mode of governance of several sovereign nations today.

To the barest minimum, ancient philosophies go as far as influencing the way people run their families. There are numerous ancient philosophies that had their periods and opportunities to run the world.

Let's take an example. Mr. Chan, a Chinese born American citizen, lives in New Orleans with his wife and kids but he still runs his family affairs and trains his children to be improvable and perfectible through individual and collective endeavors which are ideas derived from the Confucianism school of thought of the ancient Chinese philosophy.

Confucianism was developed from the teaching of sage Confucius centuries ago, that focused on developing humanness, loyalty, treating others as you would like to be treated etc. amongst other values. We are not going into further details about the Confucianism or any other ancient Chinese philosophy, as that is not within the scope of this book. This example was just to demonstrate that there is an actual philosophy that guides your daily life which you may not be able to identify or attribute like we just did with Mr. Chan and his family.

Your ancestral background may or may not determine the school of thought that you subscribe to because you probably adopted a new culture different from your original culture. You have to remember that this culture adheres to a specific ancient philosophy which may have transcended through time and numerous modifications.

How Adopting Wrong Philosophy Can Affect Life So Adversely

You would have noticed that many insurgents and terrorist groups that exist today only exist because they are guided by an enormous compendium of irrational thoughts like the belief of killing a fellow man because he chooses not to subscribe to their views. But, should that even cause a conflict of any kind?

Musa Ibrahim, a native of Northern Nigeria in Africa, was captured at a young age by an insurgent group who recruited them as suicide bombers. He and the other captives were made to believe that terrorism is a religious assignment and innocent people were killed for a good cause. They spent years in captivity going through training and several educative levels on the motives of the insurgency.

After 5 years of training, Musa was given his first, and what was thought to be his last assignment, to attack a marketplace that had about 1000 people trading. He got to his detonation point and flipped the switch, but the bomb did not go off. While flipping the switch on and off, trying to figure out what had gone wrong with the vest, he became so nervous that panic overwhelmed him and that attracted suspicion. Before he could fix the problem, he was surrounded and arrested by authorities.

Musa was leveled with several charges and was sentenced to a lengthy jail term. While doing time, a social investment and human rehabilitation organization met him in one of the prisons they visited for a program they had planned for inmates. After a long spell of discussions, they were able to figure out how he had been brainwashed and bestowed with the wrong knowledge.

Rather than further condemn him, they offered to help him. Musa was educated on reason, virtue and rationality. He was mentored on the values of life. These reshaped his life as he developed agricultural business and entrepreneurship skills as well as, a drastic change in his mindset about the essence of human life and existence. His eyes opened adequately to the wrongs he saw as right.

Today, Musa Ibrahim is a physically and psychologically different person. He is now a prosperous farmer based in the same region where he was captured. He lives peacefully with his family and with the help of the organization, he still undergoes rehabilitation exercises to ensure he does not turn back to his old ways.

Logic and rationality created a regular universal order and the source of substantial value and so, a pattern considered to be right for human existence has been formed by the philosophy and you can testify through Musa's story that there are values that you can hold on to so as to maintain and improve your rationality.

Understanding Stoicism

One of such philosophies thought to be regarded to have a significant influence on the modern-day man is Stoicism. It is regarded as one of the unique and inspiring theories that were existent during Western civilization. It is also considered as the most practical of all the philosophies.

In the bid to promote and imbibe stoic values into human affairs, Stoics shared the belief that the ultimate goal of the philosophy is for every human to experience and possess their mind serenity and the assurance of moral worth.

The Hellenistic Age (the period between the death of Alexander the Great in 323 B.C. and the conquest of Egypt by Rome in 30 B.C.) was an era of change and the philosophy of Stoicism duly exemplified the fact that expertise could be sought to any length. On the similar lines, in this modern age, knowledge and the pursuit of it has proven to burst through every form of limitation as the quest of knowledge today, has no boundaries and limitations.

There are many problems faced by the modern man that could be attributed to various causalities but this ancient philosophy has the ability to provide solutions to a majority of these modern world problems. These solutions are available at your disposal as there are steps you can take towards positively affecting your life the stoic way.

You'll learn in this book how this ancient philosophy can not only very well fit in today's circumstances; rather it will augment the pace of your growth in addressing the complexities of the modern world.

One of the primary characteristics of the stoic philosophy centers on the idea of **rationality being a unique means by which knowledge of something outside of one's self can be acquired**.

In other words, you can only gain knowledge or achieve a purpose through a rational process that will totally deter the simplest form of conflict. This explains that you can practice stoic values by tuning your mentality to a more rational mindset.

First, you need to analyze your current state of mind and your mode of knowledge acquisition. Do you only harness the knowledge you already have or do you explore for more education? This will help you understand your current reality and how to make it better using stoicism in practical manner.

Then, learn to explore rational knowledge outside the box. By doing this, you are not limited to a small cycle of knowledge for all your experiences. The stoics have hunger for learning and gaining knowledge that kept their virtue intact. Stoicism served as a way of accommodating people who believed that the success of human existence is based on reason and rationality rather than a defined and unquestioned order.

Don't Worry About Uncontrollable; Take Action on Controllable

Human being is the topmost creation of the universe, as no other species possess the level of consciousness to control and improve their lives, as humans do. However, there cannot be any denial to the fact that everything is not in our control. While we can exercise lot of control on the kind of actions we take in our life, but we can't totally control the circumstances like sudden death of our loved ones, unexpected illness despite all precautions, failing in life regardless of putting the best efforts, to list a few uncontrollable instances.

In order to grapple with such situations, Serenity prayer was evolved, which reads as below:

> *God, give us grace to accept with serenity the things that cannot be changed,*
> *Courage to change the things which should be changed,*
> *and the Wisdom to distinguish the one from the other.*

This serenity prayer was written by Dr. Reinhold Neibuhr, an American theologian, and philosopher around 1930s, which was later adopted by from Alcoholics Anonymous in 1940s.

However, the stoics already knew this principle of focusing only on things what humans can control centuries back. Stoic philosophy about being indifferent to uncontrollable and focusing on controllable things is well captured by William R. Connolly in below words:

"To avoid unhappiness, frustration, and disappointment, we, therefore, need to do two things:

control those things that are within our power *(namely our beliefs, judgments, desires, and attitudes) and be indifferent or apathetic to those things which are not in our power (namely, things external to us)."*

Nassim Nicholas Taleb in his book The Black Swan aptly describes about stoicism in this words. *"My idea of the modern stoic sage is someone who transforms fear into prudence, pain into information, mistakes into initiation, and desire into undertaking."*

The focus of Stoicism is to develop apathy and become indifferent to most situations of life, in which you can't do anything by changing your thoughts and emotions about such situation. You have to only care about the things that are in your power and on which you can take actions.

With that now let's briefly understand about the history of stoicism and its utility in the modern age before we get specifics of how to adopt stoicism in this modern world.

Chapter 1: Stoicism- How It Got Started

History of Stoicism

Stoicism is a Hellenistic philosophy that was birthed in ancient Greece. This era was during the times of so many noble philosophers who influenced various civilizations with their ideas.

The word "Stoic" has its origin in the Greek word Stoa Poikile (meaning painted porch), an open space situated in the capital city of Athens where tutors and learners often connected for the ingestive and digestive purpose of philosophical knowledge acquisition. The Stoa was generally considered as the hub of Greek civilization. It was amidst the knowledge acquisition events that occurred in the hub that birthed different stories about the fathers of many ancient Greek philosophies.

Zeno of Citium, whose parents were Greek tradespersons, was strolling through the city of Athens after suffering a shipwreck incident on his way from Cyprus. Zeno was privileged to learn from the teachings of other people in the Stoa including the Cynics; these people created and practiced Cynicism as a philosophy.

Progressively, Zeno began to ponder on the lessons he had learned and then, he started sharing his ideas with other people thereby, integrating the knowledge and insights garnered from Cynicism and different unique experiences, merged them with his thoughts and imbibe them into a philosophy that later followed the steps of his lectures. Unfortunately, not too much of his works survive, but a lot of his maxims and narratives were detailed by his followers.

The ideologies of Zeno can be defined in various forms. Note that philosophy is meaningless if it is not considered reasonably questionable, but Stoics describe the philosophy simply as a quest for happiness which can be achieved through an "ease of mind that comes from living a life of virtue in accordance with reason and nature."

The other philosophers known to have contributed to the stronghold of Stoicism are Cato, Cleanthes, Epictetus, Seneca and Marcus Aurelius who became notable after the Stoic philosophy gained momentum and crossed borders from Athens to Rome.

Epictetus was a remarkable person. Being previously slaved, he was allowed the opportunity to listen to the discussions of Stoic philosophers during servitude and after he became free, he started to give his own teachings. He is attributed accolades for his notable work on "The Enchiridion," a manual about Stoic ideas which was written by someone else. The first line attributed to Epictetus goes thus: "Some things are in our control and others not." This statement ascertains that truth directs you to the path of Stoicism.

Marcus Aurelius, who remained Roman Emperor for two decades applied the principles of stoicism in his personal life as well as in conducting the affairs of one of the largest kingdoms of that period. His book "Meditation" is a collection of his self affirmations and principles that he wrote for his personal use governing his own conduct and to lead a virtuous life.

The amazing thing about the ancient stoic literature is that though we have access to these ideas today, but many of the greatest Stoics never wrote anything down for publication. Cato definitely didn't. Marcus Aurelius never intended for Meditations to be published rather it was solely for his personal use. Seneca's letters were only the letters and Epictetus' thoughts come to us by way of a note-taking student. Therefore the philosophy of stoicism came from the people who took real actions and lead their life successful based on the stoic philosophy.

The entirety of the early Stoics developed their own ideas with Zeno's teachings through debates, arguments and clarifications amongst themselves. Those philosophical debates and back-and-forth conversations concerning the concurrent topic have endured for so many years. Champions and advocates of Stoicism are still going back and forth with themselves over the best ideas of the philosophy to be practiced.

The Modern Age

This era is the most composite and revolutionary age in world history. It marks as a significant and notable period in the development of politics, science, warfare and technology. The modern era recorded the First and Second World War first which is responsible for the origination of disordered civilization.

Characteristics of Modern Age

1. **Age of Anxiety and Interrogation:** This era was regarded as the age of anxiety and interrogation because it has most of its men and women exhibiting exceptional levels of eagerness for conjecture, research

and reorganization which you can tag as the quest for infinite knowledge. The era set an atmosphere of continual disbelief and so, requests and interrogations intensified uneven desires for a new set of values.

2. **The Transition from Art for art's sake to life's purpose:** The modern period refuted the idea of "art for art's sake" and metamorphosed it into the creed of "art for life's sake." Art and the general literature of the era became a lot more serious and more purposeful rather than just for the sake of it. It had a communal drive.

3. **Interest growth in the poor and the working class:** Some of the notable mid-Victorian writers condemned the injustice and prejudice inflicted on the poor and working classes. This interest ignited "the interrogative habit of mind" that became popular in the generation.

4. **The Influence of the Media:** During this period, the media, through radio plays and literary discourses, opened a fresh channel for authors to create their literature. This channel had an exceptional influence on its recipients. Simultaneously, bear it in mind that film techniques had their foundations set in voluminous experiments discovered in the previous literature

5. **Psychology and Literature:** The modern era birthed new psychological investigations that susceptibly influenced literature. Logical principles grew out to be justifications for emotion desires.

The modern era was the origin of the science and scientific discoveries, modernization of new values and the beginning of political mayhem and radical philosophies such as Communism, Fascism and Nazism amongst others.

Fast forward to today's world, due to radical pace of technological progress, exposure of mankind to global culture sporadically due to ease of spread of knowledge and information through internet, expansion of the business and corporate culture in a way to make the world like a small city, all that has brought in lots of chaos, fear and uncertainty in human's mind. The modern life has its own complexities due to interdependence of many factors, and also it is way more distracted than ever. A recent study by Microsoft Corporation shows that human's immediate attention span has reduced to eight seconds, that even lower than the attention span of a notorious ill-focused goldfish (nine seconds), thanks to internet and our smartphones endlessly beeping with notifications one after another. This shorter attention span and heavily distracted human attention requires a new set of training- a training to focus only on the things that are in control and become indifferent to the world's uncontrollable things- which is one of the primary teachings of Stoicism.

Let's now move ahead to learn and discuss the most common values of stoicism in the next chapter.

Chapter 2: 6 Key Tenets of Stoicism

Undoubtedly, the principles followed by earlier stoics are more than relevant in today's world, as I've explained in the previous chapters. In this chapter, we will learn about some of the most common principles adopted by the Stoics to lead their life, business and every other area of life effectively.

Let's go through them one by one.

1. Pre-meditation of Evils

This might sound contrary to the popular self-help advice of thinking positively all the time, because stoics followed the practice of thinking what could go wrong or what can be taken away from you. You love your family, parents, kids, but the hard reality of life is that someday they wouldn't be here with you or you may have to leave them behind. I know, it's too scary to even imagine that.

Today, you have good finances with you, but tomorrow something wrong may happen and you may lose all of your fortune. Your good health of today may be ruin by sudden illness or accident. Stoics followed the practice called 'pre-meditation of evils', as they believed that it helped to prepare for life's inevitable setbacks and develop resilience in the face of uncertainty.

Thinking of something wrong happening and then stressing is not what they advocate; rather they believe that one needs to be prepared for whatever happens in life. This thinking also helps to take necessary actions to avoid or delay the occurrence of such wrong things.

Seneca aptly wrote once:

"What is quite unlooked for is more crushing in its effect, and unexpectedness adds to the weight of a disaster. This is a reason for ensuring that nothing ever takes us by surprise. We should project our thoughts ahead of us at every turn and have in mind every possible eventuality instead of only the usual course of events... Rehearse them in your mind: exile, torture, war, shipwreck. All the terms of our human lot should be before our eyes."

Therefore this Life doesn't happen always the way you plan for, things can turn out to altogether different and in unexpected manner. Therefore, psychologically we must prepare ourselves for this to happen.

2. Accept whatever happens in life

Stoics had this uncanny ability to accept whatever happens in life, whether good or bad without any judgement.

Of course, we all wish that nothing bad should happen to us, but it happens, as things are not often in our control. Now what?

Can you change the past event? If you've lost a race or failed in something, can you undo the things in the past?

No. But you can change your opinion or viewpoint about the event. You can learn lesson from the past and do things differently in further, but whatever has happened, has happened already- you can't do anything except accepting the past event. Stoics called this 'the art of acquiescence', which means to accept rather than fighting for every small thing.

But Stoics went one step further, instead of simply accepting whatever has happened, they rather advocated enjoying the event. Philosopher Friedrich

Nietzsche coined a wonderful term for this known as *Amor Fati*, which means 'love for the fate'

Epictetus said: *Don't seek for everything to happen as you wish it would, but rather wish that everything happens as it actually will— then your life will flow well."*

If you accept everything that happens and rather enjoy it, then it means whatever happened as happened as per your wish. In other words, it means that things are happening as per your desire. Easier said than done, but undoubtedly, this is a smart way to avoid any kind of disappointment from the circumstances of your life.

3. The One World

One of the stoics value is they believed that the whole world is interconnected and different things are mutually dependent on other.

Marcus Aurelius wrote in "Meditations", "Meditate often on the interconnectedness and mutual interdependence of all things in the universe. All things are mutually woven together and therefore have an affinity for each other—for one thing follow after another according to their tension of movement, their sympathetic stirrings, and the unity of all substance."

Therefore, Stoics talked about common good more than individual benefit. They called this belief as 'Sympatheia' means the whole universe is mutually independent and we all are one.

If you think deeply, that's a truth. The whole universe works on the principles of interdependence between different things. Sun evaporates the water from ocean, that turn water into clouds, which in turn brings rain to nurture the soil in order to produce different crops, and that finally enables animals and humans to eat the plant and vegetables and survive.

Marcus referred to himself not as a citizen of Rome, rather as a citizen of the world. Instead of focussing solely on our own good, we all can think of great good of human race by following the principles of 'Sympatheia' in our lives.

4. Live today as if it were the last day of your life

Not in a way that you should forget everything and have total fun or joy because the world is ending for you.

Stoics believed in the tenet "Live as if it were your last day" in a different way. It's like settling your affairs well on daily basis. It's like if a soldier is going on war, he is unsure if he would return to his family or not, so he would settle all the pending matters before going – tell his children and wife how much he loved them. He knows that there is no time for petty discussions in this so short life. Stoics believe that one should live everyday discharging his responsibilities and settling the account as if today were the last day of their life.

It's better explained in the words of Seneca, "Let us prepare our minds as if we'd come to the very end of life. Let us postpone nothing. Let us balance life's books each day. . . .The one who puts the finishing touches on their life each day is never short of time"

5. Obstacle is the Way

Life is uncertain and too difficult to face often. Despite taking the best actions towards what we want to achieve, you don't know whether you will succeed or not. Also you can't control the level of hardships or hurdles that can come in your way. Stoics believed that no matter how difficult or bad situations come in their way, they had to practice their own virtues and use that situation to be at their best. Of course, you can't control the circumstance, but you can always control the way your respond to them.

In the words of Roman emperor Marcus Aurelius: "While it's true that someone can impede our actions, they can't impede our intentions and our attitudes, which have the power of being conditional and adaptable. For the mind adapts and converts any obstacle to its action into a means of achieving it."

When you choose to respond with perseverance despite resistance, you become stronger and stronger and those obstacles only become your own way.

6. Ego is the Enemy

Epictetus said: "It is impossible for a person to begin to learn what he thinks he already knows."

Stoic philosophy elaborates that ego comes in the way of your ability to learn and grow. There is no scope of any further improvement in any area of your life be it personal, relations, finance, spiritual or anything, if you already have a belief that you're perfect. With this mindset, you will be filed with false pride and won't pay heed to even the best teachers in your field to help you achieve your best potential.

Ego never allows you to reach at the apex of your chosen field in life, because you think you're somewhat superior to others. With ego, you tend to consider other people less important than you, so you are not open, flexible and willing to learn anything from others. On the other hand, treating ego as you enemy prepares you to fight any impulses or thoughts of considering yourself perfect, instead you consider yourself as a student of life and wake up everyday to embrace newer set of challenges.

Chapter 3: 8 Ethical But Pragmatic Values of Stoicism for the Modern World

The Stoics existed as a set of people who kept on a morally idealistic path while being equally realistic. Are you wondering how possible that is? But truth is that stoics had morally strong values which they followed and lived by in a pragmatic way of living. A philosopher named Charles Knapp, who was an early idealist, expressed his belief that Stoicism depicts a method through which you can look at the world and analyze all your practical and pragmatic glitches as they wield power to motivate and inspire you. Therefore, humans will continue to develop an interest in the philosophy for a more extended period.

When faced with a life barrier, stoicism makes you confidently proclaim that you will handle it in a pragmatic but idealistic way.

Key Ethical Values of Stoicism

In recent times, Stoic beliefs and values have molded up into putatively admired knowledge used to set up achievable goals. The understanding of stoicism imbibed in modern culture has beneficially clogged up in our life aspirations such that its values guide our goals.

Ask yourself these few questions:

- Do you have goals and aspirations?
- How achievable are they?
- What are your current realities?
- And lastly, what are the required principles to take in order to achieve these goals?

By the time you answer these questions in your mind, you would discover that they have a relationship with the ethical values of Stoicism that would be explained below.

These eight principles are the main ethical concepts that Stoic Philosophers and idealists held unto.

1. **Nature** – Stoicism holds that life is rational. The rationality of nature is fostered by evolutional modification. This is what propagates the value of our actions as nature has a way of inferring figurative meanings from our efforts.

For instance, there is a saying that goes; "Make hay while the sun shines." If you sift through this saying, you would understand the symbolic inference represented. It literally explains that the best time to gather hay is when the sun shines and whoever gathers hay at night risks having a moist grass.

The allegorical interpretation expresses rationality when taking specific actions, i.e., it is only rational to take advantage of opportunities at the appropriate time and not when they are unavailable. In simple terms, rationality gives meaning to life and Stoicism actively preaches this.

2. **Law of Reason** - The stoic philosophy is sustained by this concept because it explains that the universe is governed by the law of reason. There are individual rights that exist by virtue of human nature.

Usually mistaken with common law, the law of reason is known as the natural law that defines the principles of right and wrong. The principle of right and wrong is responsible for guiding your decisions. You cannot escape from the law of reason because your actions set foundations in it. For what sake do you go to work? Why do you help people? Why are you reading this book? Why do you sleep at night? These are random questions that has its responses all summed up around virtue and reason.

3. **Virtue** – Stoicism preaches that a virtuous life is one led in accordance with rational nature. Virtue is a peculiarity that is regarded to be a moral standard for excellence. As a human, you are to value this standard in order to develop as a supreme ethical being. The values that are peculiar to you are what determine your development into individual greatness and so, stoic philosophy teaches you to cultivate behaviors that eminently depict moral standards.

4. **Wisdom** - Wisdom is the essence of virtue as it is the tool used to create actions based on knowledge, understanding, insight, and experience. According to ancient Greek mythology, wisdom is said to have spawned from the head of Zeus and was humanized as Athena and Metis. The qualities of these goddesses were chastity, mercy, strength and fair judgment. The idea is a virtue that

represents and exemplifies skilled knowledge. Stoicism also instills this idea as a tool to guide your actions towards morality, logic and rationality.

5. **Apathea** – The stoic philosophy explains that your actions or decisions are not to be discorded by your passion and so, stoicism classifies passion as irrational. Of course, there are times when your desire alters your actions or make you take the right decisions at the wrong time.

   You are entitled to having your favorite hobby as playing football with friends, but that passion becomes irrational when you choose to play the sport when you are supposed to be at work. Ancient Stoics preferred to stay away from desire so as to avoid their decisions being influenced by egos and emotions.

6. **Pleasure** – Stoicism is particularly concerned about keeping virtue intact and so, it opposes anything that can affect it. Pleasure is an enjoyable feeling, but it is neither good nor bad. For instance, sexual intercourse is quite pleasurable, but Christians consider it as only acceptable when the people involved are conjugally connected. Harnessing that pleasure when not married is believed to harm the virtue upheld by Christians. And so, it merely illustrates that whatever action that you derive pleasure from, should not serve as an antagonist to your morality.

7. **Evil** – Evil is generally known as anything that lacks good in it. Therefore, it is not a far-fetched theory that anything that has the absence or opposite of good is detrimental to moral values. This idea appears to be quite broad, but it is usually narrowed to its simple term; wickedness. According to Stoicism, evil is anything that symbolizes intense

immorality. Many people often consider poverty, illness, and death as evil but they are not. This is because they do not necessarily affect your values. Poverty has no influence on your values and then, illnesses and death are more or less natural occurrences rather than evil situations.

8. **Duty** – Stoicism believes in the essence of commitment. It can be defined as a moral or ethical responsibility which every human is saddled with. The stoic philosophy demonstrates that virtue should be pursued as an obligation and not for pleasurable desires.

Pre-requisite for Harnessing Stoic Values for Modern Living

The primary essence of subscribing to stoic values is to be able to exploit its benefits concerning your way of life. Understanding the reality of following a particular belief means that you want to be impacted by the values it propagates.

To harness stoic values for your modern life, you need to set your primary life goal as being a person with a high moral standard such that challenges will have no influence on your actions and decisions.

There are obstacles you may encounter in life that will make you lose your rationality. If you have ever listened to an ex-convict or a repented criminal give a reason for choosing the path, you would realize that a lot of them indulge in the acts because of a lack of virtue.

Furthermore, you need to learn to be dutiful. This means being committed to a proper obligation. This type of commitment to duty varies from being a punctual delivery person, an incorruptible police officer, a diligent service amongst others. The essential point here is that, regardless of what your occupation is, or the difference in beliefs of the people that surround you, being dutiful is a stoic character that can be imbibed in your modern life.

Categorically, you should understand that stoicism has a straightforward impression of morality. The philosophy endorses life suitable with nature and organized by virtue. The system has an abstinent characteristic that suggests absolute disinterest for everything external as it can be either good or bad. Therefore, let your life be void of external issues that could intricate your virtue.

These values are pertinent to a virtuous modern life.

Chapter 4: 5 Realistic Benefits of Adopting Stoicism

Stoicism has so far, evidently and tremendously taught and continuously teaches us about the value of living a virtuous life, particularly in this generation that is drenched with desire and passion. The Stoic heritage continues to sculpt our world in more unexpected ways. These are five benefits of Stoicism to the modern world:

1. It Helps Get Through Hard Times

Stoicism was birthed during a chaotic period. It was conceived in Athens after the times and death of Alexander the Great which had unsettled the Greek empire into feud and disaster. The philosophy came into play as a solution to these hard times. The Stoic belief assures a life of steadfast contentment for every person that subscribes to it. It does not in any way promise substantial safety.

The Stoic philosophy illustrates that happiness is not fixed on unstable and destructible things. Many things exist in the world with an unfixed status; bank accounts, careers and even our loved ones can prosper or falter or even worse, be taken from us. The only aspect of our lives that enjoys a fixed place is our inner selves. It provides the opportunity to be virtuous, courageous, and reasonable.

The world gives all the external things we enjoy today, and so it can take everything back, but Stoicism reminds us of the inner fortress inbuilt in us. Focusing on this advantage will get you through any hard time life has to offer.

Difficult times are the reason for the stoic idea of staying indifferent on the happenings of the outside world. It is normal to languish but staying unresponsive allows you to master the art of staying equally during triumphal and disastrous times.

Although living this type of life can be challenging, it proffers liberty from passion as its reward. This way of life will allow you to be in control of things rather than being controlled by them. This does not stipulate that you should be unsympathetic. As a human being, being a stoic does not relieve you of your feelings. Instead, you only get to recognize the emotions if you choose to.

The teachings of this philosophy appear to be orchestrated to save a world on the brink of falling apart. The world today has a ton of problems ranging from finance to human relationships and peer pressure amongst others. You should practice stoicism to get through these times.

2. Stoicism Helps To Globalize Easily

The world from the ancient times till now had various menaces which it was subjected to. A lot of people subscribed to ideas that segregated race, nationality, religion, and status. People born into the stoic lifestyle will find these stratifications as bizarre.

Stoicism is the first Western philosophy to address cooperative association. The philosophy explains that we are all citizens of our world and so we should learn to be committed and responsible for everything and everyone in it. Just like the biblical catchphrase, "Be your brother's keeper." You need to embrace universal brotherhood to globalize.

The belief propagated by stoicism that our happiness is our will helps to render the majority of the social stratifications that exist, as insignificant. You should imbibe the brotherhood culture as it will help you overlook so many issues that could possibly upset you into behaving irrationally. Being a stoic will make you disapprove the divisions as it educates that people, regardless of their race, status, nationality or religion, breathe the same air.

The stoics originated a term called cosmopolitanism which plainly denotes "world-city." This term was regarded as an ideal component of Stoicism because it inspired the communalism of different races and religions. To transcend into a globalized world, you need to live like a stoic.

3. Stoicism Helps To Embrace Your Reality

One thing you should understand is that there is no perfect person and so, we all have different realities and inflated views of ourselves. These views make us feel worthy to see ourselves highly capable and above regular.

The issue with this is that our enlarged views can lead to ignorance such that we do not work towards self-improvement and that pilots us into gradually degradation while sustaining the high profile mind-set. Lack of progress leads to falling short of opportunities, relationships and other life benefits which may generate undesirable reactions in you. An inflated view of yourself shadows your reality. It masks what is happening with you at that moment.

Stoicism makes you realize the need to embrace your reality and to be honest with yourself. Understanding your reality will make you know your strength and weaknesses to grow. You will be able to evaluate your skills.

This does not signify that you should think low of yourself or see yourself as incapable of carrying out specific tasks. Instead, it makes you understand what you can achieve and what you cannot. Being imperfect is healthy and beneficial for progress.

4. Stoicism Helps To Boost Rationality Rather Than Reliance On Instincts

On several occasions, we tend to operate based on instincts rather than on rational evaluations. These instincts are usually governed by emotions. They make us develop sudden reactions to situations instead of dealing with them rationally.

Rationally attending to your situations will make you be in the moment such that your mind does not wander off to some other distorting thought. Do not focus on instincts that divide your thoughts. Instead, evaluate the credibility of the impression created out of it. Instincts orchestrated by emotions have the ability to trigger the most bias decisions under the veil of producing the best advantage for you.

Rationality helps you to build robust associations and make moral choices, as much as, your spending decisions. Distractions can lead you to make poor expenditure pronouncements.

5. Stoicism Prepares You For Leadership

This philosophy preaches us about how we can take control of situations and before we can do that, we have to master the art of controlling ourselves. Disillusionment and disappointment can truncate our chances at exercising the power of control over people and certain things. The only thing that will not let you is your self-control. It will educate you on how to manage situations irrespective of how they come to be.

Many leaders, especially the ones that have studied the ways of Marcus Aurelius and have followed the same steps, have acknowledged that cultivating Stoic behavioral traits scores them esteem and dignity in the face of failure and at the same time, it wards off every arrogance associated with one's success.

Stoicism possesses attractions for people suffering from insecurity and uncertainty. Invariably, we all suffer from that. Leaders tend to suffer more than vulnerabilities. They are usually subjected to risk and instability, and so, one way to actively regulate the imbalance is to adhere to stoic principles in order to develop the right attitude that protects and energizes the mental health.

Barack Obama once expressed his stoic character in an interview where he testified his attempt to cut down some of the decisions he has to make.

He commented that he had to reduce making decisions on what food to eat or what cloth to put on so as to focus on creating more crucial and numerous choices rather than wasting time on those.

This is worthy of emulation as you need to organize yourself. You cannot afford to allow yourself any trivial distraction. You need to learn how to draw the line between the dispensable and indispensable aspects of your life at the different levels of growth. This is the key to developing excellent leadership ability as it will keep your gaze on the essential things.

Another major challenge which we experience in our modern life is the lack of courage and selflessness. It is quite unequivocal that these challenges tend to diminish the leadership qualities that we may possess. Upholding your stoic ideal will entrust you with sufficient courage and selflessness. Lack of valor and altruism can be attributed to being the cause of our failures that seem to be more than our success.

These stoic benefits are relevant to modern life because they set you up in your realities which are void of insignificant and vague fantasies. So, you should practice being a more of a Stoic than any other philosophies as it will help you discover and accustom to the qualities such that they are subconsciously portrayed when they are needed and when they are not.

Living your life as a stoic will get you going in the good and bad times.

Chapter 5: Why Stoicism Strongly Connects with Modern Life

Our modern days are eccentric. There are so many changes that have occurred within human coexistence that have spiked some changes in the general way of life. These changes include what Stoicism has to do with men and women of the internet age. Many authors have emphasized, from time to time, on subjects concerning the Stoic notion that the philosophy is a "way of life" through their writings and other means.

Opinions have varied so far. In some situations, observers hardly hide their condescending reactions. Philosophy is referenced to ideas, the quest for real knowledge, and more recently, it has been about the uncertain hunt of cut-throat benefit in a withering space.

How would you answer if you were asked about living philosophically? Is your current life attached to a specific philosophy? Think about these questions as we move on.

Stoicism entailed a vastly methodical behavior with intentions that do not agree with the currently owned knowledge about nature. There are people who, read and follow Stoicism based on what they have found on websites, course programs and symposia and these usually clouds how they respond to academic queries from other people with opposing ideas.

Usually, the contrary opinions tend to render the idea of living as a stoic in modern times as impossible.

Why Stoicism Connects and Influences Modern Life

Is it not amazing that Stoicism, of all philosophies, has this connection? The relevance of fundamental values of stoicism has been the core for the glory of the theory, especially when studying the rundown of its history from Greece through to the Roman Stoics, Seneca, Epictetus and Marcus Aurelius.

The pertinence of the philosophy centers on some simple yet effectively instinctive and practical principles and thoughts.

These thoughts start with Epictetus' admonishment to people to learn to understand the things they can and cannot control. There is no sense in feeling miserable over an uncontrollable situation. You need to learn to focus on what you can influence. Your beliefs, present instincts and actions have to be psychologically and philosophically intelligent and advantageous.

Life would be so much easier if you worry less about all of the negative energy that people extend to you or about the things people say, think or act or even about what the future holds. These are issues that we have little or no control over. It pays to concentrate solely on the things we can presently alter.

This type of mindset will egg you on to prominent Stoic conception that your virtue or inner character is the only essential height to attain. Every other external thing, ranging from power to reputation, fame and money, should be considered as unimportant.

Here comes the value of Stoics being indifferent to external as these things are neither good nor bad, nor can they determine your happiness. Only your perception of issues has the ability to empower them. But these judgments can be tackled through practice and steadfastness.

Stoicism has been lately referred to as one of the most reliable remedies ever devised for the modern mind. However, the Stoics philosophy does not require that people be bereaved of their all for the sake of finding inner peace. Instead, it urges you to nurture your inward abilities and resources in order to enjoy and focus on your virtue.

From the times of Williams Shakespeare down to modern authors, literature has contributed to showing that Stoicism has continued to serve as one of the unshakable poles which Western culture leans on.

So far, many people may find the various qualities of Stoic ideas as alien especially as it seems that these ethics will be around for long. This insight has piloted the embodiment of Stoic principles and recommendations into 20th and 21st century psychotherapy. Observers have realized that it becomes a tad challenging to practice Stoicism rather than, just cram its theories.

We are in the times of the internet age where the true meaning and essence of privacy and other liberties are brought to book. At the same time, the internet is a significant reason the concurrent propagation of practical Stoic principles is ridded of academic evaluations.

The Relevance of Stoicism in Modern Society

Stoicism has enjoyed relevance since the wake of the modern era and it stills maintains this relevance purely because it lives by a meaningful and valuable scheme of ethics that are proficient in properly directing our engagements in tune with the modern day, despite its primal ancestries.

Stoic morals objectively enjoy an extensive scope as there is no comprehensive directory on how to live it. It is instead a combination of ideas from several philosophers whose ideas are centered on virtue, logic and reasoning. This means that the principles are justly adaptable through time and space. Understanding this relevance which teaches you some abilities such as:

- Fortitude of effort (correct labor code).

- The energetic quest for a pearl of independent and unbiased wisdom about the world.

- Decision making in accordance with reason and rationality.

- Noble conduct.

- Willing reception of constant conditions.

- The moderated tactic of intra/interpersonal interaction.

- The absence of anxiety and discomfort.

- Merry attitude towards the good and bad side of life.

The philosophy allows you to exercise absolute control on your actions towards achieving a virtuous life irrespective of whatever that could occur.

Useful Knowledge about Stoicism In Relation To Modern Life

Stoics believe that virtue is an integral characteristic of life and it is as inevitable as the laws of nature. Stoic philosophies have quite a number of specific and centralized teachings that are put in place to remind you of the random and changeable nature of the world. Life can turn around at any time such that it confers a rich person with poverty. It teaches the brief characteristic of life and how to cultivate steadfastness, strength, and self-control. Stoic ideas show a flaw in us humans as we tend to comfortably, rely on impulsive sanities rather than logic and rationality.

Stoicism does not associate with complex philosophical theories as its teachings promote actions that help us overwhelm negative emotions such that, only the necessary things are acted upon and the unnecessary ones are discarded.

The philosophy shares differences with the majority of the existing philosophies in one crucial aspect as it proposes the purposeful and practical application of ideas rather than intellectual enterprising. It is an instrument that you can use to improve the life of the modern man to become a better person in his craft and relationships with other people.

Stoics believe that certain things exist as natural and external factors to life and they should have no effect on morals. The belief explains that both illness and health, pleasure and discomfort, lack and riches, are components of life that should not have any influence on your personal virtue.

Following the principles of stoicism will give you the best chance to be able to make reasonable, well-informed decisions about your world, by focusing on objectively understanding reality and making decisions on the basis of reason. This will stand you in good stead for making wise choices.

There are specific ethics that practically set the tone for a stoic living;

- The values of justice and courage will make you gladly stand to do the right thing. Aspire to be a spirited person.

- The benefits of wisdom and temperance will make you carry out tasks and actions in ways that make practical sense, rather than, aggressive methods that lead to jeopardy.

- The absence of emphasis on external rewards will make you highly supportive of good ideas, even if it is unpopular or it comes from a person with a lesser position.

These values are very valuable to have on your side in order to settle disputes with life.

With a composed, objective worldview and a moderated approach, you will be able to manage and tackle your challenges head-on. People around you will respect you, and they are likely to find you as an excellent source of counsel and will look to you for good advice.

Chapter 6: How To Imbibe Stoic Values in Today's World

One of my many observations about the attributes of modern life is that we can easily get lost and entangled in our daily tasks, careers and moments of freedom. It is only reasonable that, as we grow and age older, we spend a better part of our available time being absorbed by the pressure of our internal and external expectations. These expectations are opportunities that are typically projected in given circumstances.

Let us take Mr. Raphael's story as an instance, he is a volleyball coach who had just been hired to coach a group of young teenagers through a regional tourney. His primary task was to train the kids through to emerging as victors of the competition. Given that, Raphael had past experience in coaching adults, he realized that coaching kids would be more difficult. Coaching the teenagers who were little and low on volleyball experience became more laborious.

In this situation, Mr. Raphael became faced with a lot of pressure that surrounded his opportunity of winning the competition. Internally, he had saddled himself with the responsibility of managing the kids to success and the external force was from people who knew him and the fame and reputation he had acquired was under review as he could not afford to lose.

Many a time, circumstances can show signs that things are not going well and so it leads to fretting, anxiety and stress. This is why we get angry and aggressive when things seem to be beyond our control. It is important to be watchful of these emotions to manage the reactions of other people efficiently. This is a crucial factor in ensuring and maintaining a reliable, optimistic and virtuous character.

This chapter is aimed at helping readers understand the principles of stoicism and also to practice Stoic teachings and reflections to discover its multiple advantages concerning modern life. The philosophy is quite consequential to the modern age as it offers solutions to many problems that we encounter today. Thus, it is regarded as the KEY TO MODERN LIFE.

Stoicism places its central attention on the **simplicity and moral nature of life** meaning that to live completely happy and positive in this era, you need to develop a sound and virtuous character. You have to put in a conscious effort into upholding a rational personality as it guarantees you excellent mental state.

Your mental state is the most pertinent part of the stoic mind as it is the personal version of yourself that requires full concentration. It has to be adequately preserved from the wrong stimuli in order to be truly happy and contented with life. This is the reason for the reiteration of the salient stoic idea of getting rid of external issues and focusing on the inward. You need to focus on the inner you.

Stoicism as a key to modern life seems quite logical, but are you thinking about it? If you are, to what extent? One of the major problems of the modern age is that we share a false communal belief that possessing numerous material properties will earn us respect and approval from the peer or that it will grant peace of mind. But the hard truth is that the life works from inside-out, and not the other way round. Once you have mastered your inner state of mind to lead a virtuous life, and focus on taking action on things that you can control, the outside world doesn't matter. You only focus on doing the right things and become indifferent to the results, because you understand deeply that you have control only on the actions, and results will only follow if the actions are put in the right manner.

How To Imbibe The Values Of Stoicism In Modern Life

Let's now understand some of the practical ways to imbibe the values of stoicism in our modern lives.

- **Develop A Mindful Attitude**

This is a practical way to master the art of living your modern life stoically. Developing an attitude to usher the activities of your day is one smart move to make towards living a life of virtue. Seneca once included in one of his writings of how short life is. Understanding that should always remind you always to remain watchful of all your daily actions. Living mindfully means merely organizing your day according to a thoughtful plan.

Take Jessica's fabulous day for an instance, she wakes up early enough to observe a morning run to invigorate her body and work her heart to pulsate correctly for the new day. She loves to read in the morning on her way to work to procure new ways to improve her creativity and to also inspire her mind for positive and inventive thoughts that are advantageous to her career.

All the conversations and interactions engaged in are directed towards resourceful topics whether in a written or social milieu with the mind throttled on the type of person she dialogues with, probing into their character for the sake of understanding them genuinely. Jessica is mindful of her nutrition as she organizes them to the right time. All exercises and meditations have their periods set in some alone time spent after work.

There is a predominant factor that circulates all of Jessica's daily activities. All her actions are focused on improving her inner self. This is an example of the mindful attitude to be developed for your modern life. This does not necessarily mean that you have to organize your day into Jessica's order. Instead, you should plan your activities to your satisfaction without trampling on your virtue.

• Focus On What You Can Control

There are so many events that have been pre-ordained to occur on a regular day and it is accompanied with some which you can control and others which you cannot. Usually, a lot of us spend quality time doing the most irrelevant and unproductive undertakings. We often allow ourselves to be stressed by things we already know about. Getting worked up over predicted traffic which you already expect is retrogressive.

There is a solution to this; you have the ability to modify your tactic to daily activities such that unnecessary daily stress is totally avoided. For instance, it is wiser to have a raincoat in your bag or an umbrella in your hand when going out on a gloomy day so that you do not have to worry about getting drenched when the rain starts.

Whatever event that occurs in your day which you have no control over should be rendered as void so that it does not get the chance to disrupt your day. One of Epictetus' quotes goes, "It is not the things themselves that disturb people but their judgments about those things."

This quote explains the magnitude at which your judgments contribute to your daily glitches. You need to learn to use your ability of cognitive evaluation to decide the important things to focus on.

- **Prepare For All Outcomes**

More than a million issues are happening daily which are definitely going to have outcomes. How do you deal with the differences? When going for a job interview, you should have it in your mind that there will be feedback from the interviewers. It could be positive or negative. Whichever way, you have to station your mind towards any result.

These outcomes possess the capabilities to invoke different emotions. Getting rejected by a job interviewer will make you sad and being awarded a contract worth an excellent pay will make you elated, but one thing you should always keep in mind is that it could have gone either way. This will enable you to feel less disappointed with many of our modern problems. An unfavorable outcome is what condemns people into giving up on themselves when they really need to push more.

Being in the right mind for all outcomes will give you a resilient spirit and it will guarantee your continuous triumph over your challenges.

- **Cultivate A Philanthropic Behavior**

This stoic attitude does not necessarily imply that you have to hand out banknotes to the less privileged or that you have to give all your earnings to other people whether they need it or not. Instead, this suggests that you should live a communally beneficial lifestyle. Some people are bereaved by sad situations, abusive relationships, physical and verbal abuses and other menaces on the list of emotionally draining events.

These events are part of the reasons stoicism has proved to be very instrumental to modern life. Being philanthropic means, you can alleviate people of their pain. You should learn to extend comforting hands to people who need it. It could be through comments and compliments.

One time, I was seated in a bus with a lady who seemed quite dejected. I could not really ask her what was wrong, but I did something to help her situation. I merely slipped a note into her palm. It reads, "You are as beautiful as the day, you will be more beautiful when you smiled." After she had read it, I noticed her chin go up uncontrollably into a ravishing smile. I felt a lot more fulfilled afterward than any other thing I accomplished that day.

Chapter 7: Effective Practices to Become a Modern Stoic

Stoicism: More than Just a Theory, Practice It

Many cyber societies share the prevailing opinion that Stoicism is beyond technical evaluations. It is an actual way of life and should be imbibed into modern day culture. Here are some tentative steps that should be practiced:

Meditation

This is one of the many stoic principles staying at the heart of today's Stoic revival. It involves recommendations that may be identified by several people as "spiritual exercises" that consists of pensive and thoughtful activities in which you are encouraged to envision your circumstances in order to examine them from a larger viewpoint.

Stoic Meditations involves the exercise of recollecting and premeditating, from time to time, on how you will confront the day ahead, the people who misconstrue you and conditions that may not be in your favor. This exercise allows you to bear in mind that the thoughts that drive your actions are your primary concern and it is best to focus on using them to create the right activities rather than stress on how people have wronged you.

For instance, Seneca teaches that meditation should be done every night, before sleep, in order to adequately analyze all of the actions of the day in the perspective of Stoic philosophical principles so as to easily discover the errors and ensure the absence of repetition subsequent days. Therefore, you should often meditate, in order to envision your next steps towards preserving your virtue.

Maintain Philosophical Journal

Philosophical journal is different from your regular journal. Unlike your regular journal, your philosophical journal is where you write down things that happen during the day. You write down what happened to you and you also analyze how you responded to these situations.

You note down how you reacted to people's input, as well as how you viewed situations. By doing so, you become aware of your mental and emotional patterns. You start seeing problem areas, but you also start seeing areas where you can take full control.

This can pave the way for you developing certain habits that would enable you to practice more personal control, regardless of what's happening and your external circumstances. By writing this down, you can see your progress. You can also analyze things that you may have completely overlooked, if you did not write them down.

Intentionally impose discomfort to your Body

Don't allow your physical body to be too much comfortable, rather expose yourself to physical discomfort to a certain degree. One example could be to follow a one day fast during a week. When you let go of food for at least one day on a regular basis, you not only toughen yourself up mentally and emotionally to physical deprivation, you also access a tremendous amount of health benefits.

Another example is to park your car far away from the market when you go to buy grocery. This will force you to walk more than usual, and when you come back with hands filled the grocery items, you will have to walk longer. Again this is to mentally and physically improve your stamina, so you don't start complaining when you have to face adverse situation i.e. you don't have you car with you or you are forced to walk longer in emergency situation.

Living like a Stoic

The answer to the question asked earlier in this chapter about how a person would know that they are living philosophically or particularly like a Stoic is clear. Living like a Stoic simply implies living ethically according to the principles of the philosophy.

These practical ethics include:

- Living dutifully.

- Envisioning every day before it starts and when it ends.

- Psychologically preparing for setbacks.

- Acting based on logic and rationality rather than impulsive sanities.

It is a well-known fact that the majority of the 21st century people now identify with modern Stoic societies. This suggests that many are beginning to understand the benefits of the philosophy in addition to the knowledge that its ancient mission is idolized to transcend through time immemorial into several stages of academic recapitulations.

Further tips on living like a stoic

- **Avoid self-centeredness and work hard**. This will garner respect and value for you from other people as you will be of substantial assistance to their growth.

- **Accept the unalterable**. This will enable you to go through life with less squandered energies and reduced disappointments. Focusing on unchangeable situations will only lead to wasted efforts and discomfort and so it is advisable to focus on accepting and learning from such conditions.

- **Do not place your delight and dignity on external factors** that create happiness through material things and vain objectivities. Living like a stoic will give you satisfaction and reliability as it generally has a criterion that maintains your moral conduct and absolutely keeps it under regulation.

- **Be willing to help always**. This is an efficient act of making a valuable person of yourself and to other people. It attracts positive energy towards you, and it makes you want to do more.

Practical Stoic Exercises

Perform early morning reflections

It is essential to understand that you need to perform early thoughts on your life. This activity is actually more distinctive than planning how to run your day. It is more about immediate steps to take that will be of immense benefits to you now and in the future. This will enhance reactions to what you do during the day and to the actions of other people that may concern you.

Firstly, you should learn to be grateful for the benefit of life and the privilege to wake up every morning to new opportunities of life which many other people may not enjoy.

Then, strategize on how to clinch to your virtues and escape from your iniquities. Choose a particular personal strength you can build and rely on and look for ways to imbibe it into the day. Prepare a mental solution to possible situations that may occur during the course of the day.

Always jog your memory to solely focus on the fact that you can use your thoughts to influence your actions. Only attempt to control what is in your capacity.

Practice physical self-control

This useful practice entails an intentional act of restraint in some of your physical activities. This involves denying yourself some things that give you pleasure for the sake of getting a value off it. In a way, this may seem like a negative foresight as it involves you purposefully exposing yourself to hardship in order to prepare you for the negative occurrences that may arise in the future.

This practical exercise gives you the ability to withstand hard times.

Exercising conscious self-control will develop you not to crave things that are beyond your reach as you may not be able to control them. Do not forget that you should only focus on what you can control.

This exercise will also enable you to hold loosely onto the things of life such that the impact will be light if you lose it. Life can be likened to sand. When you hold tightly onto it, you tend to lose your grip of it.

For instance, abstaining from carbonated drinks that contain high sugar content and only drinking water for a while will train you on how to separate your satisfaction from such beverages.

Self-control is pertinent to living well as it gives the chance to perceive everything as temporary. All the things that exist today will exist no more sooner or later. So you should view and act on life as if you were borrowed. Therefore, losing a valuable possession should not affect too much or for too long.

To practice this, deny yourself of internet access for a specific spell of days or leave your car at home and use public transportation to your destinations. You can also effect some alterations to your daily activities that may seem slightly uncomfortable.

Practice late night evaluations

This particular exercise should be your last activity before going to bed. It is a cross evaluation of the things you had previewed in the morning before stepping out for the day. The difference between this and your early morning reflections is that, instead of examining what to do as an antecedent of what is yet to happen, you will be evaluating the events that have already occurred.

This will help you realize the mistakes you have made and pave a way to prevent them in your future actions. By practicing late night evaluations, you need to have a psychological rerun of how your day played out and check through with some questions such as:

- Did I live the day in relation to my beliefs?

- How did my interaction with people go today? Good or bad?

- What previous errors did I attempt to correct? Was I able to?

- Did my virtues make me better in any way?

The response to these questions will reveal the aspects of your life that you have to keep up and the ones you have to improve. This will also adjust your plans for the forthcoming days. During these reflections, you can create a list of your daily goals, and you check them from time to time after completion.

Your notepad should contain practical things that you wish to affect with changes irrespective of how small or how meaningless it may seem. Also learn to understand that the losses you suffered during the day cannot be recovered and so since you have no control over them, you need to accept the reality, ignore the lapses and move on to the next achievable objectives. Basically, you should always look forward to learning from your mistakes.

Conclusion

As you have already learned in this book that despite Stoicism being an ancient philosophy, it doesn't lose its significance to operate the modern world in the best possible way. Instead by following the values and principles of stoicism has a strong potential to augment the quality of life in this chaotic and complex modern world.

You learned about the key tenets of stoicism, and how stoicism connects well with the modern world environment. Therefore, we can easily conclude that stoicism is quite germane to help human being thrive in this modern era. As a Stoic, you will come off as a happier person and the people around you will be glad to interact with you. Your positive impacts will make you a contagion of good energy. You will be more productive in your harmonious space.

We all have heard that knowledge is power, but without implementation of the knowledge, you can't see the effects of that power. If you don't implement what you know, it is as good as you don't know the stuff.

Therefore, it is the time to start implementing what you have learned. The practical exercises stated in this book will help you get started towards a better life.

Wish you a happy life full of wisdom and joy.

Disclaimer

While all attempts have been made to verify the information provided in this publication, the author does not assume any responsibility for errors, omissions, or contrary interpretations of the subject matter herein.

The views expressed are those of the author alone and should not be taken as expert instruction or commands. The reader is responsible for his or her own actions.

Adherence to all applicable laws and regulations, including international, federal, state, and local governing professional licensing, business practices, advertising, and all other aspects of doing business in any jurisdiction in the world is the sole responsibility of the purchaser or reader.